TO THE WOMEN

DONNA ASHWORTH

From The Author,

Women, we are intrinsically connected like the moon and the ocean, nothing creates more powerful waves than a group of females in sync.
I found out many years ago, that a life without a sisterhood, could be one, could be two,
could be fifty,
is a life lived lacking.
We need each other on this rollercoaster ride.
When women support women, incredible things happen, right?
Thank you for opening these pages and for being 'that woman'.
The kind of woman who wants to inspire others; be a cheerleader, a confidante and a place to go to when the world seems dark.
Thank you also, if you have bought this book as a gift, for that is what I really made it for, to pass along and bring some light, some solidarity, when someone needs it the most, or perhaps just in case they ever may.
If you find something worthy within my words, I would love to hear from you. It inspires me to keep going and to keep growing.
All the very best to you,
Donna
X

CONTENTS

CONTENTS (Continued)

Shine your brave light BRIGHTLY & your people will find you

BE THAT WOMAN

Be the kind of woman you want to call when things go wrong.

Be the motivator, the encourager of dreams.

Be the kind of fierce friend you want to have yourself.

Love your girlfriends deeply, they are your sister warriors in this
world
and only they know just what a crazy, hormonal ride womanhood
really is.

Be loyal, love hard.
Be a soulmate, be a sister.
Be strong, be kind.
Listen hard, laugh lots.
Tell the truth but keep the secrets.

Bring light to everyone you meet, kind words travel endlessly.
If you can't say anything nice don't say anything at all.

Spread the sparkle of a smile and a compliment whenever you
can.
There is room for us all to be happy and successful.
Lend a hand if you're there already.
Pull your girls up, push them if you need to.
Straighten each other's crowns, spot the lipstick on the teeth
and the loo paper on the shoes.

Avoid the drama, smile at the haters,
they're actually your biggest fans.

IT'S TIME

There comes a day, somewhere in the middle of every woman's life, when Mother Nature herself stands behind us and wraps her arms around our shoulders, whispering,
"It's time."
"You have taken enough now. It's time to stop growing up, stop growing older and start growing wiser – and wilder.
There are adventures still waiting on you and this time, you will enjoy them with the vision of wisdom and the companionship of hindsight, and you will really let go.
It's time to stop the madness of comparison and the ridicule of schedule and conformity and start experiencing the joys that a life, free of containment and guilt, can bring."

She will shake your shoulders gently and remind you that you've done your bit. You've given too much, cared too much, you've suffered too much.
You've bought the book as it were and worn the t-shirt.
Worse, you've worn the chains and carried the weight of a burden far too heavy for your shoulders.
"It's time" she will say.
"Let it go, really let it go and feel the freedom of the fresh, clean spaces within you. Fill them with discovery, love and laughter. Fill yourself so full you will no longer fear what is ahead and instead you will greet each day with the excitement of a child."

She will remind you that if you choose to stop caring what other people think of you, instead of caring what you think of you, that you will experience a new era of your life you never dreamed possible.
"It's time," she will say,
"to write the ending, or new beginning, of your own story."

TO THE WOMAN WHO THINKS SHE ISN'T GOOD ENOUGH

To the woman who looks around and wonders, why everyone else
is so much more capable,
so much stronger, so much more ambitious, than her.

To the woman who thinks everyone else is blazing a fiery path
through this thing we call life, while she limps behind, barely
getting through the days. Somewhere, another woman is looking
at you thinking exactly the same.

You see, we all look like we're kinda nailing it, from the outside in.
We all look together sometimes. Catch us on the right day and
hey, we look like we have it all.
Because guess what, we learned to look that way a long time ago.
We learned to hide our struggles behind a smile and whack on
that mask every day.
And actually, we are doing each other a favour when we show up,
just as we are, warts and all, late, flustered, human.

What we really need to see is that we are all the same. We all
struggle.
We all fall apart.
Some days we nail it, other days we get nailed.
By hiding our own weaknesses, fears, worries - we give them more
power. If you let it out, shine a light on it all, it becomes so much
less scary, funny even…
And goodness only knows we need to laugh.

So, to the woman who wonders if she is good enough…
If this is you. Yes you are. You always were.
You don't have to live up to everyone's expectation of how you
should be coping.
You are human, flawed, wonderful, miraculous, loveable, loved.
I see you,
Now do me a favour and go see all the others too.
Spread the word, we are good enough, just as we are.

WHEN YOU SAY GOODBYE TO A PARENT

You are suddenly living in a whole new world. You are no longer *the child* and regardless of how long you have officially been *grown up* for, you realise you actually never were, until this moment. The shock of this adjustment will shake your very core. When you have finally said goodbye to both your parents, you are an orphan on this earth and that never gets easier to take, no matter how old you are yourself, and no matter how many children of your own you have.

You see, a part of your body, and your soul, is fundamentally connected to the people who made it. When they no longer live, it is as if you are missing something physical you very much need. Because really, you are. You are missing your parent and that is something far more necessary than any limb.

And yet, mystifyingly, the connection is so strong it carries on somehow. In some way, shape or form they are still guiding you if you listen closely enough. You can hear the words they would choose to say to you. You can feel the warmth of their approval, their smile when a goal is achieved, their all-consuming love filling the air around you when a baby is born they haven't met.

If you watch your children very closely you will see that they too have a connection with your parents long after they are gone. They will carry on traits, thoughts and sometimes they will even see them in their dreams.

This is not something we can explain, love is a very mystical and wondrous entity.

It is far better to have loved and lost, than never to have loved at all and grief, grief is the price of that love. The deeper the love the stronger the grief.

When you say goodbye to a parent, do not forget to connect with that little girl who still lives inside you somewhere.

Take very good care of her, for she, she will be alone and scared. When you say goodbye to your parents, you lose an identity, a place in the world. When the people who put you on this earth are no longer here, it changes everything. Look after yourself the way they looked after you and listen out for them when you need it the most. They never really leave.

DEAR FRIEND

I'm sorry for being so bloody rubbish.

But you see, life moves really – really – fast.
From the minute I open my eyes there are some small people,
several big people and even some animals who are relying on me
for many different reasons.
Some of them involve eating and basic survival.
I am spinning plates and dropping plenty.
You, my dear friend are one of those plates.

But I love you very much.

I wish that every text message I wrote to you in my head made it
into the virtual space and into your phone, to let you know you're
in my heart and on my mind.
I wish I could carry through with all the plans we make, knowing
we never will. I go there in my mind – it's loads of fun.
When I drop, frazzled, into bed at night, I remember I haven't rung
you, again.
Then I remember I haven't locked the back door or brought the
cat in and just like that, it's happened again and I have forgotten,
again.

I am very hopeful that one day life will be easier and we will be
blessed with plenty of time for laughing, talking and sharing.
Stick with me,
I promise I will be worth it – when we are old and grey and you
need someone to laugh with in the nursing home.
I'm there.

Yours Loyally,
Your bloody rubbish friend.

YOU CAN'T BE EVERYONE'S CUP OF TEA

There will always be someone in this life who just doesn't like you,
no matter how hard you try to please them.
There will always be something that you say, or do, which causes
offence or division.
Whether you meant to or not.
There will always be someone who finds fault in you, your life or
your words.
You may never find out why.
Please don't waste your precious time trying to.

You cannot be everyone's cup of tea.

Then there will be those who like you on impact. A little fizz of
energy that passes between you. Silently, unseen, bonding.
Those people will not only like you but they will like you fiercely.
They are your people. Whatever spare time you have, spend it on
them.

You cannot be everyone's cup of tea, but you can be someone's
first sip of a cold drink on a sunny day.

Or a warming hot chocolate when you come in from the rain,

Or the pop of a long awaited champagne cork,

Or a stiff shot of tequila when things go awry.

Find your people,
love them hard.

TO OUR DAUGHTERS

You were born made of softness, sweetness and love, but with a will so strong it could bend iron – despite what society may tell you, you don't have to lose one or the other.

Your super-power in this life, is that little voice inside of you that tells you when something isn't right, listen to it.

Your self-worth is controlled by you, only you. Never put it in someone else's hands.

You are equal to, (not better than), anyone else you may ever come across in this life.

Never lose your joy. No matter how serious your ambition, or how driven your path is, remember we are here for only a short time and life is to be lived.

Comparison will not propel you ahead, rather it will keep you back from the real treasures in this world. Stop comparing. Better still, never start.

Fear is an instinct but unlike your inner voice it can be misleading. Never let fear hold you back from the wonders you could see.

Do not let society, or anyone, tell you what beauty looks like. If you feel beautiful, you are. If you see beauty, it's there. Your beauty is an amalgamation of everything that makes you you, and it is utterly unique. Embrace that, early.

You don't have to choose between being a warrior, a princess, a lady or a woman. You can be all of them in one and most women are, every day.

Lastly, it is okay to not be okay. It is even better if you talk about it. Darkness cannot shine through light, but light can shine through darkness. You can be amazing and admired whilst admitting your weaknesses and discussing your fears and anxieties.

Even more so in fact.

Oh and....never let anyone dull your sparkle,

you were born to shine.

you
can be
SOFT and
STRONG
you don't have
to choose

ONE DAY

An army of furious older women will take over the world...
And I want to be there at the front.
Because one day, every woman wakes up and realises, that quite
frankly, they put themselves through hell.
Trying to fit in, trying to be enough, to be attractive, to be
acceptable, to be responsible, to be reliable, to be a mother, to
be a wife, to be a friend, to be a carer, to hold a career, to keep it
all spinning effortlessly…
And in a flash, years and years of back-breaking conformity,
whizzes before your eyes and you have a lightbulb moment…

It was never going to happen.
We could never have done it all.
For it is not possible.
No man could do it either.
Not a chance.

Women of this world, beautiful, wonderful women,
let that lightbulb go on sooner rather than later because when it
does,
you will be free.

Free to live.
Free to f up.
Free to take breaks and make mistakes.
Free to pass over on the list of things you 'should' be doing.

And you will understand that whatever you did today, it was
enough.

You are enough.

One day, an army of furious older women will take over the world,
and I want to be there, right at the front.

THE GREYS, THE DIMPLES, THE ROLLS, THE WRINKLES

The greys, the dimples, the rolls, the wrinkles,
Don't strip you of your grace.
The lines, the weight, the clothes that pinch,
Don't steal light from your face.

If you could see what I can see,
Your world would open wide.
The way your smile lights up the sky,
The soul you have inside.

The greys, the dimples, the rolls, the wrinkles,
Don't wash you of your wonder.
The lines, the weight, the clothes that pinch,
Aren't worthy of your anger.

If you could see what I see now,
Such beauty carved through time.
You'd grieve the years you missed that joy,
The tears and wasted time.

The greys, the dimples, the rolls, the wrinkles,
Don't steal away your light.
But the way you talk down to yourself,
Those harmful thoughts, just might.

THAT'S ALL YOU

Somebody somewhere smiles when they hear a song
that reminds them of you.

Somebody somewhere laughs when they recall a joke,
you once shared.

Somebody somewhere feels good when they see your name
light up their phone.

Somebody knows they have a safe place to go to with
you, should they ever need it.

Somebody is comforted by the thoughtful little gift which
you gave them.

You matter.

You have created an invisible network of
thoughts, emotions, feelings, love and friendship,
which spreads so much further than you realise.

You.

That's all you.

When you embrace
your own
flaws
someone watching
finds their
way

BY 40 YOUR MIDDLE FINGER IS AT HALF-MAST

By 50, it's full on UP.
By 60, both of those fingers are hoisted in a V…and not a single care is given any more.
I mean, we care about our family, our friends and our passions.
We care about the environment.
We care about equality and living in peace.
But we don't care about 'fitting in' and we don't care about what people think of us.
Not anymore.
Too many years were wasted on that.
We certainly don't care to stay quiet, or bite our tongues – we haven't wasted all these life lessons, to play dumb when the situation calls for our wisdom.
Hell no.
Neither do we care if our waistline is the acceptable size or if our thighs are toned and unblemished.
We have wrinkles, we have stretch marks, we have war wounds, warts and all.
And we are rocking each and every one of them in all their glory.

You see, there comes a time in every woman's life where you realise that this is it.
This is the time to be alive.
To live without restriction or oppression anymore.
To break free of the chains society binds us with and tear loose.
This is our time to be completely and totally who we were supposed to be all along.
The sooner you get there, the better.

Life waits for no woman.

THERE WILL BE DAYS

There will be days, my friend...
When you feel like you just can't go on.
Just keep swimming.
Breathe in and breathe out and wait for the light of a new day to
dawn.

There will be days, my friend...
When nothing seems to be making sense.
It's not supposed to.
Clear your mind and open your heart, the answers will come in
time.

There will be days, my friend...
When the pain rises up and engulfs you.
Be kind to yourself.
Lay low and let the tears flow like a river, release, open the
floodgates, let it out.

There will be days my friend...
When it feels like the whole world is against you. When it feels like
you cannot do right for doing wrong.
Just sit it out.
Tomorrow is a new day and these feelings will pass. I promise.

You see, life is all things, from one day to the next.
It is beautiful at times, wondrous, amazing and joyful - then it is
awful, miserable and heart-breaking.
And the cycle goes around.
It is as it should be.
Everything is as it should be and you, you will be okay.
Have faith.
Keep hope in your heart.
Tomorrow is a new day.

10 THINGS TIME HAS TAUGHT ME

1. Most of our life is spent chasing false goals and worshipping false ideals. The day you realise that, is the day you *really* start to live.

2. You cannot please all of the people *all* of the time. Trust your intuition and don't fear putting yourself first occasionally.

3. Fighting the ageing process is like trying to catch the wind. Your body is changing, but it always has been. Don't fight futile battles, instead change your mindset to see the beauty in the new.

4. Nobody is perfect and nobody is truly happy with their lot. When that sinks in, you are free of both comparison and judgement.

5. People watching you are mostly looking for faults, when you realise this, you will stop wasting time chasing perfection and instead chase your own truth and accept your shortcomings.

6. You will regret the years you spent berating your looks, the sooner you can make peace with the vessel your soul lives in, the better.

7. Your health is obviously important, but stress, fear and worry are the most damaging poisons. Happiness and peace are the best medicine.

8. Your love and your wisdom will live on far longer than any material thing you can pass down. Tell your stories, they will travel farther than you can imagine.

9. We are not here for long but if you are living against the wind it can feel like a life-sentence. Life should not feel like a chore, it should feel like a wonderful adventure.

10. Always, always, drink the good champagne and use the things you keep for *best*. Tomorrow is guaranteed to no one. Today is a gift that's why we call it the present. Eat, Drink & Be Merry.

IF I COULD WRAP YOU UP AGAIN

If I could clear your path of stones,
And break the sticks to save your bones,
I would.
I would.

If I could lay your way with flowers,
And bring you sunshine every hour,
I would.
I would.

If I could shield your heart from pain,
And give you strength to rise again,
I would.
I would.

If I could take those from your life,
Who tear you down and bring you strife,
I would.
I would.

My child it's hard to let you go,
In a world so full of hate and woe,
And though I know it must be done,
You'll always be my little one...

If I could wrap you up again,
And kiss your cheek to ease the pain,
I would.
I would.

YOU WERE BORN WITHOUT A WORRY

You were born not caring much,
For the curves along your thighs.
And it took you several years
To care a thing about your size.

When you die, I'm kinda thinking.
That your thoughts won't stray to that.
You won't waste your final breath,
To utter words of being too fat.

Yet the years spent in-between,
From your birth till you depart.
When your life is there for living,
When you're young, alive and smart.

Are the years you waste with worry,
For the way your nose sticks out.
Or the changes in your body,
You can't do anything about.

And those years may seem a-plenty,
But for some they end too soon.
What if you had not embraced them,
Whilst your world was in full bloom.

So, remember how you frolicked,
Little child of untamed glory.
It's not too late to change your thoughts,
Not too late, to change your story.

YOU STARTED WITH A BLANK CANVAS

Beautiful, unspoiled, that much is true.

Then life began to mould you, shape you,
draw its art upon your skin...
Stretch marks, freckles, sun-spots, wrinkles, laughter lines and
frown lines.
And every time something new appeared upon you,
you mourned the loss of the smooth, unspoiled and innocent.
What you failed to recognise is the beauty of your journey,
the true strength of your fight, is now etched upon you for
eternity.
You are a work of art.
A work of learning.
A walking story.
A beautiful, broken warrior.
Your body, and you, have been evolving since the day you were
born and will do so until the day you die.
Don't fight it.
It was always meant to be so.
If you must change something, change the way you see it my
friend.
Change the way you see it.
There is much beauty you are missing.

REMEMBER HER?

Somewhere inside of you, there's a little firecracker with her arms folded and a frown on her face.
She isn't happy about all the times you said no when you wanted to say yes.
All the times you said yes when you wanted to say no.
She wanted you to buy the ticket.
She wanted you to take that trip.
She definitely wanted you to take that risk – the one that may have just opened a whole new world.
She wants you to remember what it feels like to run to the sea without a care in the world and splash and laugh till you ache.
To face the day without a fear in your heart and embrace every opportunity that comes.
She doesn't understand why you won't wear the bikini.
She doesn't understand why you won't eat the cake.
She doesn't understand why you don't let it go.
She definitely doesn't understand why you accept second best.
Somewhere inside there is a little girl who wonders at the adult you've become..
She still has many things she wants to learn and so many people still to meet.
She still has food she'd like to taste and parties she wants to dance at.
She still has places she wants to visit and wonders she wants to stare at.
Somewhere inside you, there is a little firecracker,
desperate to see more of this thing we call life.
Go get her, she's fun.

IF YOU ARE A WOMAN WITHOUT HER MOTHER

There will never be a day you don't miss her.
Never a day, where you don't wish you could hear her voice or ask for her advice just one more time.
There will never be a moment that you don't regret all the times you screened her call, or missed a visit, simply because life was just too busy.
And now you realise busy is fake, it isn't real.
She was real and she is gone.
And you are alone.
And the feeling of abandonment and loneliness is huge. Mind-blowing, no matter how loved or surrounded by family you may be.
None of it is her.
When the woman who brought you into this world is no longer here, it is a lonely place.
And you are now she.
You are now the one expected to guide, to discipline, to love, to handle everything, for everyone. And that is a shock.
But you got this.
Because she taught you well.
She made you right and she made you strong and she filled you with enough love to share around, even after she was gone.
So go on.
And make her proud.
And remember, look out for the little girl who still lives inside you somewhere, she misses her Mama very much.
Be kind.

DEAR FRIEND,

I don't need you at your best when you come to my home.
I don't care what you're wearing or what car you drove here.
I don't care if there is food on your shirt or if your hair has not
been brushed.
None of that matters to me.
I care about you.

I care about what's in your heart, how afraid you are, what you
worry about in the night.
I care about your deepest fears and your biggest dreams and I am
there for it all.
If you mess up, I won't judge.
That's my promise to you.

So, don't cancel me because your house is a mess and your
cupboards are bare.
I will bring what you need with pleasure and I will listen to your
problems without measure.

If you are on the floor, I'm picking you up, or I'm sitting right down
beside you.
You need never be alone down there.

And before I leave, I will have made you smile at least once.
That's my promise to you.

So, save your best for someone else my friend,
because I want you just as you are.

That's what friends are for.

TO THE WOMAN WHO IS SLOWLY FADING AWAY

To the woman who has lost her spark.
To the woman whose get up and go, has well and truly gone.
This is for you.
This is to remind you whose daughter you are.
This is to remind you, that you don't have to be everything to everyone, every day.
You didn't sign up for that.

Remember when you used to laugh? Sing? Throw caution to the wind?
Remember when you used to forgive yourself more quickly for not always being perfect.

You can get that back again.
You really can.
And that doesn't have to mean letting people down or walking away.
It just means being kinder to you, feeling brave enough to say no sometimes.
Being brave enough to stop sometimes.
And rest.

It starts the moment you realise that you're not quite who you used to be. Some of that is good, some of that is not.

There are parts of you that need to be brought back.
And if anyone in your life is not okay with that… they are not your people. Your people will be glad to see that spark starting to light up again.
So, if you have been slowly fading away my friend, this is the time to start saying yes to things that bring you joy and no to things that don't.

It's really pretty simple.

AGEING ISN'T ABOUT LOST YOUTH

It's about finding...

Who your true friends really are.
The difference between shiny and worthy.
The confidence to be yourself in any room.
The time to dedicate to the things that bring you joy.
The wisdom to say no to the things that don't.
The freedom to choose your own path in life.
The courage to be happy in your own skin.
The knowledge that very little really truly matters in the end.

Ageing isn't about lost youth, my friends,
no… it is not.
I haven't lost a thing, in fact.
Except perhaps, my ability to give a toss, about the things that
won't matter when I'm gone.
And remember, not everyone gets the chance to grow older.
It truly is a privilege denied to many.

No, ageing isn't about lost youth,
It's about finding,
who you were meant to be, all along.

don't change
the way you LOOK
change the way
YOU SEE.
There is much
BEAUTY.
you are missing

THERE WAS A PHOTO OF A WOMAN

There was a photo of a woman on the internet,
She was smiling as she splashed amidst the sea.
I read the comments underneath and this is what they said,
"Her body is just way too big for me."

There was a photo of a woman on the internet,
She was laughing and dancing, life seemed good.
I read the comments underneath and this is what they said,
"That girl needs to eat some fattening food."

There was a photo of a woman on the internet,
She was asking everyone to buy some shakes.
I read the comments underneath and this is what they said,
"Yes please, help me lose this awful weight."

There was a photo of a young girl on the internet,
A mother's post, to say that she had passed.
I read the comments underneath and this is what they said,
'Why did she suffer, why did she not ask?"

I see so many photos on the internet,
And everyone has something bad to say.
And I was thinking, maybe, it's our words which need to change.
Maybe, we should find a kinder way.

RIGHT NOW, YOU'RE SOMEBODY'S HERO

Today, remember that the bad times are part of your journey too.
They are part of your story.

So own them,
never let them own you.

These challenges that you face?
You are 'supposed' to be facing them.
You are 'supposed' to come out victorious.

This is just another chapter in your book.

Never underestimate the power of your hardships, they will inspire others,
they will create waves that ripple on for years.
They will help others to face their own – and come out fighting.
You see, it's not just the good chapters of our stories that people will want to read about.

We all need a hero to look up to.

Right now, this stuff that you're dealing with, makes you somebody's hero.
So put on your cape and get it done girl.
Then shout it out from the rooftops that you survived.
Your story could be someone's saving.

GUT FEELINGS ARE YOUR GUARDIAN ANGELS

Listen very closely to those little feelings that start in your tummy
and try very hard to be heard.
They are the voices of those who watch you.
They are your guardian angels doing their thing.

Pay attention to the hairs that bristle on the back of your neck.
For when that happens, you have been touched from above by
someone who has your very best interests at heart.

What is it they heard that made them connect?

Go back, find it.
Listen.
If you are struggling to make a decision my friend...

Say it out loud as though you were talking to a loved one and wait
for the feelings that follow.
You are never, ever alone.
You are always being guided in everything that you do.

Likewise, when your instincts are screaming at you to leave, to free
yourself, to move on to better things.
Listen hard.
They are right.
Pay close attention to the voices deep inside.

They are your guardian angels.

Let it go
you need
that SPACE
for something
far more
wonderful

WHEN YOUR HEAD HITS THE PILLOW TONIGHT

Remember the smiles of the day, the laughter, the little wins, the warm words…
And let everything else go.

Put the lessons learned in a file marked 'done' and give yourself a pat on the back for the things you got right.

Leave the stresses of tomorrow where they belong – tomorrow.
Leave the stresses of today where they belong too.

And let the night take away the heavy weight from your shoulders.

Let it go.
Let yourself be safe.
Let yourself be still.
Let yourself be at rest.

When your head hits the pillow tonight my friend, let sleep come and let your soul be.
You did enough today.
We are all just doing our best with no rule book, in a game with no referee and no half-time.

None of us are getting it right, we are all just winging it.
We are all just as scared, just as weary.

When your head hits the pillow tonight my friend,
 close your eyes and remember, you are worthy.

WAVE THE WHITE FLAG

There are many choices available to us women in this life – but when it comes to your body, there are only two:
Accept it
Or don't.

You see, if you choose to accept your body, you will soon start to love it, admire it, look after it.
These things all follow in the wake of your acceptance.
When you realise that this vessel for your soul, for your spirit, is an instrument of such high design and fine tuning that it boggles the mind to even think about, you will enter into a phase which I like to call 'peace, at last'.

You will care nothing of spare fat, grey hairs, loose skin.
You will realise, eventually, that the body's purpose is not to look good, to attract friends, partners, successes – that it is, in fact, your spirit which does all of those things.

If you would only allow it to shine through and work its magic.

Your body, my friends, has but one job, to see you safely through this adventure of life, to allow your spirit to reach its potential.
That is it.

If you are on the path of not accepting your body, you are in for a very long battle, against an enemy you have no power to defeat.
Nature, time, biology, fate…
You don't have the weapons to fight those powers.
Wave the white flag.
Give in.
Accept.
It is then that your life will truly begin.

THERE WAS A TIME

'There was a time I would' have set myself on fire, to keep others warm...
'There was a time, when I would' have crossed oceans to reach people who wouldn't cross a stream for me.
'There was a time when I would' try, too hard, to be seen by those, who would simply never see me.
'There was a time, when I felt' myself unworthy of a person, who could actually never be worthy of me.
But not anymore.
You see, my friend, there are many ways to spend your time on this earth – but wasting it on those who are not worthy of your attention, is a crying shame.
Use your time wisely.
Save your best efforts for those who care. For those who would return the favour, who will appreciate your attention. Those who truly value you.
And the rest? If they do not see you now, they never will.
And they are missing out.
Make this the time that you realise your time is precious and should only be bestowed on those who bring you comfort, positivity, support, love or joy.
Or all of the above.
Remember, you are the main act, not a warm up, and this, my friend, is no dress rehearsal.
This is it.
The curtain is well and truly up.
Shine on.

look how far
you have come,
you are a
WARRIOR
and you are
NOT DONE YET

TO BE A WOMAN

"What's it like to be a woman?"
A little bird whispered in my ear.
"Is it just like being human?"
Oh it's so much more, my dear.

We are the holders, we are the keepers,
Of the secrets and the truth.
We are the safe place in a storm,
The creator of all youth.

We are the place where life is softest,
We are the colour in the story.
We are the wisdom and the instinct,
Mother Nature in all her glory.

We are the taker of all worry,
We keep it deep within our hearts.
So that others may unburden,
So that great new lives may start.

We are the makers of the home,
Not just the walls but of the spirit.
Bringing everyone together,
Letting love and laughter fill it.

We are sisters, mothers, wives,
So many things in every day.
We are the start of every life,
We are the reason, we are the way.

We are fuelled by intuition,
Call it magic, if you like?
We are truly so much more,
Than any words that I could write.

YOU'RE GOING TO LOSE PEOPLE ALONG THE WAY

And it will hurt like hell....
You're going to lose people along the way,
People you thought you'd never lose.
People you truly believed would always be there.
And it's going to hurt like hell.
But that, my friend, is life
People change, relationships change. Some evolve. Some
disintegrate.
Some people leave through no will of their own and that hurts the
most. They didn't want to go.
But you, you will survive it all.
You will.
You will look back and realise that the people you need, really
need, are still here, in some way.
And that the other relationships you lost along the way, have
taught you something that made you better.
And that's life.
Hold close those, who are in your life now, and remember the
ones who left, fondly. Even the ones who broke your heart.
Regret nothing.
Use the feelings of pain, to commit to a life here and now, a life
where you take no one or nothing for granted. Where you cherish
every minute with those people you love.
You're going to lose people along the way, my friend.
But that is life.
Every minute counts.

THERE'S A WOMAN IN MY MIRROR

There's a woman in my mirror,
And she looks a lot like me,
Though there are lines around her eyes,
And her hair is wild and free.
She is plumper than myself,
And she is definitely grey.
Did I miss the day this happened?
Has she always been this way?

And this woman in the mirror,
Has an air of something calm,
Like a tide that's going out,
And a beach that's soft and warm.
She has seen the world in colour,
She has learned to know the truth.
There's a wisdom in her wrinkles,
There's a knowledge brought from youth.

And she seems to move more freely,
As though released from earthly binds.
Is she made of something lighter?
Perhaps the weight she left behind.
Like the press of expectation,
And the need to yield and bend.
I like this woman in the mirror,
She's fast becoming my best friend.

YOU WEREN'T BORN TO FADE AWAY

Life may smooth away all of your rough edges, with its twists and turns and lessons to be learned.
Life may force you to fashion a tough outer shell.
Life may break you and reform you many many times, until you don't even recognise the shapes you see in the mirror anymore.
And that's okay, it really is.

Just don't let life make you smaller.

Don't let anyone convince you that your cracks, your scars, are a sign of weakness.
They are war-wounds, my friend.
Battles fought and survived.
They are your story, your fight, your journey.
Let life reshape you over and over again, sure, but don't let it make you fade away.

Fading away is not what you are here for.

Let peace fill your heart as the years go by and your wisdom abounds.
Let anger and pettiness fall from its pedestal.
But don't let your voice diminish.

There are countless young women out there who need to hear you and hear you loudly.
You weren't put on this earth to burn brightly then fade away, my friend.

Get louder.

You have much more to say now.

IF YOU WOKE UP TODAY

If you woke up today with a mountain in your way,
And your energy has all got up and gone.
If your heart is set to break and the stress you just can't take,
Let the world around you march and carry on.

Don't be scared to take a seat and to admit a short defeat,
It's not wrong to lose the will once in a while.
Let your body shed its weight, give your mind a tiny break,
Let your thoughts flow free, breathe deeply, find your smile.

You only get one time alive and it's vital that you thrive,
You're a living breathing human full of wonder.
You need water, you need sun, you need food and you need fun.
You need to take time out to charge or you'll go under.

It's not you who's full of fault, it's the world which needs to halt,
Don't confuse your weary heart with something broken.
We all keep a too-fast pace, this is life, it's not a race.
Listen hard my friend and hear the truths I've spoken.

SET IT DOWN

You must feel so heavy,
With the weight of all that expectation.

Set it down.

The guilt,
The worry,
The fear,
The comparison.

It's too heavy.

Set it down.

You can't reach for anything new if your hands are full of
yesterday's trash.

So,

Set it down my friend.

It was never yours to carry anyway.

THAT'S FRIENDSHIP

Be there for the messy parts of someone's life.

Don't be afraid of the ugly

Hold someone's hand when no one else can,
Or will.

Pull them to stand.

Be there for the dark moments and then enjoy the light together.

Don't take a seat at a celebratory table, if you you won't be there
to collect the shattered pieces when that same world falls apart.

That's friendship.

It's easy to get an invite to someone's pretty, someone's
celebration, but if you get invited to someone's raw and real.

Show up,
you have been blessed.

tomorrow the

SUN

will rise again
and so, my
friend will
YOU

MAY

May your days be filled with laughter.
May your chores complete themselves.
May your mind have time to wander.
To a sandy beach of shells.

May your morning stretch be graceful.
May your lunch be full of taste.
May your inspiration find you.
May no moment go to waste.

May your lonely days be lacking.
May your friendships linger strong.
May your thoughts be full of wonder.
May your worries all be gone.

May your money flow like water.
May your problems float away.
May your needs be met and more so.
May you wake to sunny days.

May you find the strength inside you.
May you learn to look within.
May you see yourself more kindly.
May that journey now begin.

IF I EVER HAVE TO LEAVE

If I ever have to leave you love,
Please know I didn't choose it.
You were my every waking thought,
My world, I wouldn't lose it.

If I ever have to leave you love,
Don't think I didn't fight it.
If I had any choice at all,
We would never be divided.

If I ever have to leave you love,
I truly rue the day,
I always thought I'd be with you,
Beside you, come what may.

If I ever have to leave you love,
Please know I'm always there.
That somehow I will find a way,
To show you how I care.

If I ever have to leave you love,
The one thing you must know,
Is that you meant the world to me,
I didn't want to go.

If I ever have to leave you love,
You'll always have my heart.
Never fear, my soul is near,
Even when apart.

If I ever have to leave you love,
Try to hear my laughter.
And see my smile once in a while,
Let me live with you hereafter.

THE ART OF AGEING GRACEFULLY

Think about it, you have earned this face.
Every line, a laugh shared.
Every wrinkle, a year survived.
Every age spot, a day that the sun shone on you.
Some women believe that as they age, they lose their looks. Oh my friends how wrong this is.
A beautiful young women is a happy accident of nature but a beautiful older woman?
She is a work of art.
The Japanese have a practice whereby they fill any broken objects with gold, believing that something which is broken has earned its beauty and should be celebrated and decorated rather than discarded.
I feel this way about women.

It took a long time to find out who you really truly are. A long time. The acceptance that old age brings is freeing. It brings with it peace and happiness.
Everyone knows, happiness looks good on us all.
Your body has been changing since the day you were born and will continue till the day you depart. Ride with it, accept it, embrace it. Be amazed by it.
Allow your face to represent your life, your stories, your joys.

Why choose to be an older woman fervently chasing youth, when you could be that older women who knows what she is worth and has earned every minute of her hard-won self-acceptance.

The trick with ageing gracefully my friends, is to pay as little attention to it as possible.

PERFECTION is a myth which we must stop believing in

NOW THAT I AM OLDER

The list of things I want, has grown smaller with every passing year.
These days, I can pretty much narrow it down to,
good health for us all,
enough money,
enough time,
enough fun,
enough adventure,
enough work,
really, just enough.

Enough.

That's really all that I want.

The list of things I don't want, however, has grown bigger, a whole lot bigger.
At the top of that list comes unnecessary drama.

As I get older, I realise that I can handle pretty much any negativity or adversity life may throw my way.
But I don't have to.
I don't have to sign up for it all.
It's pretty freeing.
In fact, I can cancel my subscription to anyone's drama, anytime I please.
And I have.

If it costs you your peace, it's too expensive right?

Spend wisely my friend,

Life is short.

TO THE WOMAN (OR MAN) WHO WILL LOVE MY SON ONE DAY

It is hard, so hard, to imagine a day where I will not be the moon,
the sun and the sky to my little man.
When he is sad, he calls for me.
When he is scared, it's me he needs.
When he feels excited, I am the one he rushes to tell first.
I am the keeper of his secrets, the finder of anything which is lost
and the solver of any known problem in his little world.
I am his everything and he is mine.

One day, you will have the pleasure of being his everything.
One day it will be you that he comes to, and that is, of course, the
way it should be.
But I wonder if you will ever think of me sometimes, perhaps let
me be the first to share some good news – or allow me the honour
of pulling you both out of some trouble life may throw at you.
I will be waiting, ready and willing.
I will not meddle or fuss or pull you in opposite directions I
promise you that, and should you be blessed with children of your
own, there will be no one, no one on this earth who will love them
more than I.

The bond between a mother and a son is divine, this much is true,
but I wish for him the very same bond with you.

And I pray the circle of love goes on and on and on, much further
than me.

After all, that is what I brought him up to do.

Love.

DEAR WOMEN

Maybe you don't know, just how amazing you are?
Maybe you don't see how you keep everyone going,
even when you're struggling yourself?
Maybe you don't realise how much cheer you bring others,
regardless of your own level of happiness?
Maybe you don't see the smiles you spread, or the joy you bring?
Maybe you don't know what an amazing effect you have on the
world you created?

Well you should know.

You are the kind of women we all need when things get hard.
You hang on, when the wind blows, and even better than that, you
keep others hanging on too.
You, my friend are a wonderful creation.
How do I know this?
Because your ability to inspire and support other women, brought
you here somehow.
Maybe you were given this by someone who sees this in you.
Or maybe you are reading this book because you found it
somehow, whilst your shining light was attracting other bright
flames, like a magnet.

You are wonderful.
You should really see that.
I do.

you are not
broken
you are
broken open,
that's how
LiGHt
gets in

GETTING OLDER

Is like being given a Backstage Tour.

Without the lights, the sets, the music - suddenly you see the whole production for what it is... a show.
You catch a glimpse of the 'star', without make-up, getting ready to go home - and you realise she is not the superhuman entity you thought her to be.
She is just a person, like you.
They all are.
We all are.
The dressing rooms smell of sweat and the costumes need washing.
The sets are made of wood and hollow in the middle.
Reality exists in every corner of every life, no matter how glamorous the facade.
Getting older, is like being given a manual on life, decades too late, or perhaps, right on time?
Suddenly it all makes sense and you will no longer focus or pay attention to the wrong things, the false idols.
Getting older is being given the gift of time, even though time is running out, you value it so much more that every minute is worth a hundred.
Getting older is a privilege denied to many...
Grab it with both hands and seize not just the day, but the seconds.

HAVE THE COURAGE

Have the courage,
To live as a whole.
To listen to your heart,
To talk to your soul.
To know who you are,
When others do not,
To look out for vibes,
To filter your thoughts.

Have the heart,
To appreciate life.
To laugh and to cry,
To accept both are right.
To go with the flow,
When the winds of change rage.
To learn to let go,
To break free from that cage.

Have the vision,
To share your own story.
The ugly truth heals,
As much as the glory.
Pass down your lessons,
The joy and the pain.
Remind those who follow,
To dance in the rain.

Have the patience,
To wait for the signs.
But never stop living,
enjoying the ride.
Listen to silence,
As loud as the screams.
Respect life's sorrows,
Follow your dreams.

THERE WILL BE SOME VERY PAINFUL MOMENTS IN YOUR LIFE

There will be some very painful moments in your life, my friend.
There will be moments, days even, when the sun doesn't seem to
rise in your world. When food has no taste, the world has no joy
and everything seems like an effort too far.
Yes, my friend, there will be some very painful moments in your
life.
But you will get through them
'This too shall pass.'
Because life has a way of throwing you a rope, just at the very
moment when you thought you couldn't go on.
All you have to do is grab it.
Then one day, as is the way of this life, the sun will suddenly beat
down on your face again and the air will feel fresher than it ever
did.
And there will be laughter. And love. And joy. So much joy.
And life will be sweet, like summer after a long winter - a winter
that was so dark, each colour that appears, feels like the first time
you are seeing it.
This is when you must live. Really live.
For, just as the bad times do not last forever neither do the good.
'This too shall pass.'
But that is life.
So, embrace the joy when it comes and let fear slide away. And
when the dark times come around again, remember you have
what you need to survive. And you *will* survive my friend. You
really will.
Keep the important people close and focus on what truly matters
and you will find yourself dragged to safety, each and every time
the storms come.
And on those days, when your sun is high in the sky but you notice
another facing bad weather, you drop your raft and you go to
them.
And if they won't climb in with you, to safety, you simply stay with
them in the stormy water till the sun rises again.
And it will, it always does.

FOLLOW ME

"Follow me", she said,
"I'm going somewhere new.
It's not a place on any map,
it's deep inside of you.
You can't get there by car,
or boat or any train,
You get there just by feeling,
by switching off your brain.
It's far beyond the madness,
buried deep beneath your fear.
Under all the doubt and worry,
further still,
you're near.
Once you're there,
please be prepared,
you won't want to come home.
As you realise heaven was inside you,
hidden,
all along."

YOU WON'T FIND MY WORTH IN THERE

Don't define me by my size,
You won't find my worth in there.
See no measure in my thighs,
Or the colour of my hair.
Don't judge me on possessions,
Or the holidays I take.
Don't wonder of my treasures,
Or the money I may make.
I'm a mixture of emotions,
All rolled into a form.
Full of life and love and laughter,
And memories so warm.
I'm all the lands I've wandered,
And the stories that I've read.
I'm all the thoughts that visit,
When I rest at last in bed.
I'm a complex mix of lessons,
Which I've learned along the way.
I'm an echo of my musings,
And the things I didn't say.
I'm often fiercely happy,
And sometimes deeply sad.
I'm kind and deep and loving,
For that I'm truly glad.
So look at me and wonder,
Of all that's deep inside.
Don't just assume you know me,
And the stories my smile hides.
If you take the time to delve,
You will find out more each day.
But for now no need to judge me,
Till you've walked with me some way.

don't live
your life
against the wind
let go
see where
you fly

CHANGE THE WAY YOU SEE

I don't have crow's feet,
I have happy happy memories of laughing with friends until the
tears flowed.

I don't have frown lines,
I have the marks of my frustration and confusion – which I battled
through – smiling in the end.

I am not going grey,
I have shimmering highlights of wisdom, dashed throughout my
hair.

I don't have scars,
I have symbols of the strength I was able to find, when life got
tough.

I don't have stretch marks,
I have the marks of growth and the marks of motherhood. My tiger
stripes of love.

I am not fat,
I bear the evidence of a life filled with abundance, blessings and
good times.

I am not just forgetful,
I have a mind so full of stories, memories and moments there is
scarce room to hold much else.

I am not old,
I am blessed – with a life of great length – something not
everyone can say.

Don't change the way you look my friend, change the way you
see.

WHAT IF?

What if you're never ready?
What if, this is as close to being ready as you'll ever actually be?
What if, the biggest regret you have when you look back on your life, is that you wasted time waiting, waiting to be better, when you were already so very much enough?
What if, the last thought you have when your life comes to an end, is that you didn't do enough living whilst you were alive?
My friend, this is it.
This is your life, right here, right now.
And let me tell you something...somebody somewhere went to sleep last night assuming tomorrow would be a new day.
And it wasn't.
Today is the day.
Every day is the day.
Life waits for no one.
Seize the moment, seize the day.
Dance like nobody's watching.
Watch the sunset.
Eat the delicious cake.
Put your bare feet on the cool grass.
Be alive.
Be ALIVE.
Put your hand on your chest and feel that heartbeat pulsing through your body.
That's all you need to be ready.
That is truly all the purpose you ever really need.
You, my friend, are alive.
So live.

Thank you for reading my second book, perhaps you have read some of these pieces on my social media pages over the years, or maybe these words are all new to you? Either way, I hope you saw yourself in here at points. One thing I have found over the years is that we women, regardless of our differences, have so very much in common.

If you care to follow me at Ladies Pass It On, I would be very pleased to have you. I have been amazed at how many amazing women have supported me and my words over the last few years, it is something I will never stop being grateful for.

Donna x

Manufactured by Amazon.ca
Bolton, ON

35573319R00068